Dawn has come

RESOURCES

The inner way: a mystic anthology of songpoems, stories, reflections (SRP, 2013)

Tuppany series
* *Wake up! if you can: sayings of Kabir*

Dawn has come

songpoems of Paltu
translated by Anthea Guinness

 SALT RIVER

TUPPANY

is an imprint of Salt River Publishing
a Division of Wowkay Enterprises, LLC
Phoenix, Arizona
www.SaltRiverPublishing.com

First edition
16 15 14   7 6 5 4   III II I
ISBN 978-0-9893349-3-8

All Salt River books are available through
www.SaltRiverPublishing.com/estore/

CONTENTS

v

A word on style

- Most of the songpoems in this book are *kunɒlis,* a circular style of poetry that brings about a sense of intensity and then completion (the second half of the first line is echoed in the first half of the second line; the whole of the first line is repeated in the last line, bringing the poem full circle). They are sung to a beautiful haunting melody, which is used only for Paltu's *kunɒlis.*

- In the western secular world, we are more comfortable referring to teachers of the past like Moses, Krishna and Jesus without any title, as also with saints like Kabir, Rumi and Paltu. No disrespect is intended.

INTRODUCTION

In the 1500s in a small village in northern India –
Peeran Kaliyar near Saharanpur – there lived a
mystic known simply as *bheekh*, "mendicant". One
day, wandering through a market in Delhi, one of
Bhikh's disciples kept repeating his master's name,
intoxicated on love for the master.

"Yaa Bhikh! Hail Bhikh! Yaa Bhikh!"

The local qazi, a magistrate trained in Islamic
law, stopped the man and said, "Listen, you
non-believer, what is this nonsense you're repeat-
ing? Say the name of God, say the name of the
Prophet, but what are you repeating *bheekh* for?"

Then he asked him, "What is your name, my
man?"

"Bhikh."

"What is the name of your God?"

"Bhikh."

"Who is your Messenger?"

"Bhikh."

A crowd had gathered by this time and they dragged the man to the mosque to set him right and make him recant such heresies.

At the mosque, the disciple went on repeating "Bhikh" in response to the questions he was asked. The elders declared the man to be a *kaafir* or non-believer – a crime punishable with death by hanging.

In those days nobody could be hanged in a religious case without the approval of the emperor. So the accused man was taken before Akbar the Great. At a glance Akbar could see the man was an intoxicated faqeer and his punishment was unwarranted. Akbar asked the same three questions, and Bhikh's disciple continued to answer "Bhikh".

Akbar then asked, "How about getting your master to make it rain and put an end to this drought we are having?"

The disciple said, "I'll ask him." The emperor asked, "When?" "The day after tomorrow" was the man's reply.

Akbar gave orders for the man to be released. The elders objected, saying he would just disappear. The emperor said, "No problem. Let him disappear!"

The disciple went out into the jungle and sat in meditation, contemplating on his master. Will of the Lord – it rained. The following day he went to the court of the emperor. Akbar said, "It rained!" The disciple replied, "Yes, thanks to my master."

"Ask for your reward," commanded Akbar. But the disciple said, "Apart from Bhikh, I don't need anything, Sire."

Beckoning to his minister, Akbar dictated and sealed a gift of twenty-one villages in the name of the mystic Bhikh. Then he handed the document to the man and told him to deliver it to his master.

Everybody was surprised when he handed it right back to the emperor. "With all due respect, Sire, he won't be interested. Villages are worldly wealth. Property like that is meaningless to him. Forgive me, sir, but I couldn't present him with a document like this."

So the emperor sent two men instead to deliver the document to Bhikh. (Whether he refused or accepted, we can only guess.)

A few days later the disciple went to visit his master. Bhikh immediately said, "Tell me, what did you ask for – *rain!* You could have asked me for anything – to make you a saint, a Friend of God, or anything else, and I would have given it to you… At the time you were sitting in contemplation of me, I was sitting in contemplation of my master and his court!"

The disciple said, "Hazur, what do I need with all that? I only need one thing: You."[1]

This is the lineage of Paltu. Paltu and his master Gobind were successors in the line of Bhikh of Saharanpur, Uttar Pradesh – masters of Shabd, the Word, and Naam, the Name, judging by what Paltu put into writing.

And judging by the names of these mystic teachers, the Saharanpur lineage transcends religious backgrounds entirely: Bhikh is a Muslim, Gobind a Hindu, and Paltu we know was born into a Hindu family.[2] Other Naam bhakti lineages show the same "mixed" religious backgrounds – Kabir, for instance, was a Muslim but chose Dharm Das, a Hindu, as one of his successors – all of them having numerous Muslim as well as Hindu disciples, as did Paltu, Gobind and Bhikh.

The beautiful songpoems of Paltu are a record of the teachings that Paltu and his predecessors lived, exemplified and shared with the seekers and disciples of their day.

The selections in *Dawn has come* make no attempt to represent the full range of the mystic teachings Paltu wrote about, which are covered elsewhere.[3] The focus is rather on the characteristics of a bhakti master and the unfolding of the inner path. Paltu's songpoems in this collection paint a picture of the master/disciple relationship, the love and devotion of disciple and master, and give glimpses of who the true master really is.

The roles of a master

The living master is the core of the Naam bhakti path. In this particular form of mysticism, "devotion to Naam, the Name," one of the master's roles is to link the seeker to the Word or Name – the mysterious power of God that creates and sustains the creation. Referred to as Word, Name, Command, Voice, Truth and numerous other terms in the sacred traditions of the world, the bhakti mystics commonly call it Shabd (word, sound) and Naam (name).

In one of his songpoems, Paltu emphasizes the importance of the relationship between disciple, master and Word in order to safely cross "the ocean of existence" and return to the source – without drowning in the attractions and temptations of the world:

> You want to know how to cross
> The ocean of existence?
> You need to search for a boatman
> Who knows the secrets.
> Step on board the boat of somebody
> Who understands the mysteries
> Of both harbour and high seas.
>
> Travellers who climb aboard
> The boat of Word with full attention
> Will safely reach the far shore
> Without getting their feet wet.

But first, says Paltu the slave,
Make sure of the teacher –
Then go ahead, feel free to cross
And land on the other side
Of this ocean of existence.[4]

The Naam bhakti way of spiritual evolution
is through connection with Shabd or Naam, the
dynamic reverberant divine creative power that is
within everybody – but remains unperceived in
most of us. As Paltu suggests in this songpoem,
Shabd is the vehicle that transports one through
the stages on the inner journey. And the master
of Shabd, the Shabd master, is the captain.

In another songpoem Paltu shares his experi-
ence of Shabd and its transformative effect – how
this divine energy brings about the death of the
ego and gives new life and liberation to one's semi-
dead consciousness, taking one to full spiritual
realization. He says:

"Shabd removes desire for kingship, turns you into a faqeer, a lover of God – turns you into a lover of God and leads you to the Lord. When Shabd takes hold, nothing else pleases you. Only if you die from the wound of Shabd, do you really come alive. …Wounded, you wander – it gives a heavy blow, this Word. Death comes to you while you're alive: you're spent, thrown away – and then you get up, completely taken care of, set right. Paltu, whoever is wounded in the heart by the arrow of Shabd finds that Shabd removes desire for kingship and turns you into a lover of God!"[5]

Elsewhere, he speaks of the transformative effect of that same divine creative sustaining power, this time calling it Naam, the Name: "Through the power and glory of Naam, I have been totally, but totally, transformed! Now all I can do is fall at the feet of the Great One. What can poor sesame oil do – in the company of fragrant flowers, it's sold for a fortune! The saints are full of mercy and compassion: it's they who have made me like themselves. …I belong to the lower class and I was a mine of impurities, but through the power and glory of the Name, I have been totally, but totally, transformed."[6]

The mystics say it is necessary to be connected to the inner current of the divine power and guided on the inner path by somebody who knows everything about the way – a saint or true master, a *satguru* or *murshid-i kaamil*. Paltu says:

> They alone can merge us in Naam.
> They are the experts –
> They show us the path to union.[7]

By definition, the true Naam bhakti master is God-realized, at one with the source of the Word or Name, the Lord, yet alive in the world as a human being that people can see and interact with. Paltu describes the mystery of the master's state of inner realization in several songpoems, including this one:

> Millions of ages, millions of dissolutions –
> Throughout them all I was the Maker.

> I was the Maker –
> The creator of the Creator!
> At the very beginning, I alone was:
> I am the one who is called Creator....

> Paltu, I do not die.
> Only the wise will understand.
> Millions of ages, millions of dissolutions –
> Throughout them all I was the Maker.[8]

As a master, his tasks include teaching and exemplifying a pure way of life, linking disciples with Shabd or Kalma, the divine Word, showing them how to meditate and encouraging them in the on-going practice. In one songpoem, for instance, Paltu advises his initiates to close the doors of the senses when they meditate and to penetrate deep inside the eye centre or window in the sky where they will hear the inner sound and go beyond duality:

"Tell your desires: Be quiet, be still! Close eyes, ears, nose and mouth, my friend – then you'll see the radiant light and you'll open the window in the sky. With the path through the window before you, go ahead, step through – you'll hear the sound of *haq, haq,* the resounding of Truth. Annihilate twoness and in this way yourself become One."[9]

By living the disciple's way of life and practising meditation, the disciple develops inner concentration and experiences the current of the Word or Greatest Name, Ism-i Aazam – which is manifest within everybody as resounding sounds and radiant light,[10] as Paltu mentions in his advice to initiates.

At an advanced stage of inward focus and concentration, the disciple's consciousness merges with higher and higher frequencies of the Word – described by Paltu in one songpoem as "going from palace to palace" within.[11]

Paltu hints at the type of spiritual teacher required for this when he says: "The melody from the skies of Gagan, the peak of the mind's realm – whoever brings that is my beloved master! Yes, that is the divine master and he is the one I will serve."[12]

In a songpoem urging people to meditate and find the Beloved within themselves now, while they have the chance, he advises: "Play the game of love for the whole of spring, says Paltu. When the end comes, it will be too late to regret. Foolish one, why are you fast asleep? Spring is passing you by and the Beloved has not yet come to your home!"[13]

The living master

All bhakti mystics say that without a living master, there is no path. Paltu is uncompromising on this point. He says that God is everywhere, so finding God is easy; but unless you find a mystic teacher to put you on the inner way and guide you to God-realization, then "God won't be enough" – that omnipresent quality of the divine will not enable you to attain to spiritual wholeness and union:

> Finding God is easy –
> It's finding a saint that's hard.
> And unless you find a saint,
> Says Paltu, God won't be enough:
> You'll never be complete.[14]

Why is it hard to find a saint? First, because most of us are convinced we do not need any help or intermediary, especially a mere human like us, to reach God. We are perfectly sure we can travel the spiritual path to God-realization on our own, through our love, personal practice, religious commitment and spiritual beliefs.

Second, the saints are hard to find because they are hidden. They don't advertise, and never have. In the modern era, they often refrain from making their books available commercially; they generally do not give interviews on radio or TV, nor do they participate in religious conferences.

Yet when the masters wish, they reveal their presence to sincere seekers, wherever they may be in the world. A seeker may spend years searching, attending meetings and reading, feeling restless and dissatisfied, longing to find something that brings confidence and inner peace. As it happens, the path of love is a path of surrender; the challenge even at this preliminary stage is to accept the timing and know that when the master sees the seeker is ready, as the mystic saying goes, he will appear.[15]

When somebody does come into the company of a true master, Paltu says they are transformed spiritually. Using a series of playful, ironic analogies, one Paltu songpoem conveys that the transformation is inevitable and profound.

Inadvertently, the songpoem also gives a glimpse of Paltu's love for the masters and his own sweet sense of humour.

The songpoem begins: "Anybody who comes into the company of a saint or listens to his discourses is ruined, absolutely spoilt, like cheap oil permeated with the fragrance of flowers!"

After a series of examples, the unexpected ending emphasizes the complete transformation brought about by the master's company:

> This black crow Paltu
> Has turned into a swan
> And now all the crows are commiserating:
> I warn you, friends –
> Anybody who comes
> Into the company of a saint
> Is ruined forever![16]

Introduction

One of the reasons the masters take birth as human beings is to experience what ordinary people face in contemporary life and show by their example it is possible to lead a family life, earn one's living, deal graciously with life's challenges – and still make the spiritual practice one's top priority.

In one way or another, the masters gain our attention and then speak about the path, answer questions, talk about the spiritual potential everybody has and show how to achieve it. Paltu explains: "A tree doesn't grow fruit to feed itself, a river doesn't drink its own water: saints take on a human body for the sake of others."[17]

Paltu's songpoems convey a vivid impression of what an inspiring, impelling, attractive presence the living masters are in a disciple's life. Without that magnetic presence of the master, the path would be dry, tasteless and overwhelming.

As Paltu says in "Soothing as sandalwood," the masters through their human presence make the path possible: "His gentle voice and loving words melt stone, turn granite into water! The way he lives, the way he walks, the way he smiles, bring fragrance to the path of enlightenment."[18]

In these lines Paltu captures a sense of the charismatic effect of the living master – as do these other lines from "Soothing as sandalwood" and "So tender, soft":

Soothing as sandalwood,
    serene as the moon:
The saint is like that. Soothing, serene,
He puts out the burning of the world.
If anyone comes to him on fire,
    all they need
Is the sweetness of his face, the sound
    of his words.[19]

So tender, soft –
No one but the saints is like that!

You can't hold a candle to them –
They are kind and compassionate
To all without exception.[20]

Paltu conveys the characteristics of a true master – his unconditional love for all, his tranquillity, forgiveness and patience. But he also paints physical details that take his writings from the abstract to the lyrical in a way that anybody who has witnessed the effect of a living master can relate to. In "So tender, soft," for example, clearly referring to memories of his own master, he says:

Friendly, smiling, his sweet words
And a voice that catches your heart
Thrill people with delight,
Leaving them overjoyed
As he passes, serene,

His glance showering jewels
Of grace and good fortune.[21]

Who or what the master is

Paltu's songpoems describe the mystic or God-realized saint in a variety of ways – sometimes from the point of view of a seeker, sometimes from the point of view of a love-intoxicated devotee, and on rare occasions from the supreme point of view, revealing who and what the true master eternally is.

In one such bold utterance, Paltu starts the songpoem by apparently speaking of the Lord:

I was in the beginning,
I shall be in the end:
My fragrance dwells in everything.
I am the one who lives in everything –
Nothing else besides that.

By the end of the songpoem, however, it is clear that Paltu is speaking of the master – in fact, of himself:

> Paltu, because of this human form
> He is the Lord, I am his slave.
> I was in the beginning,
> I shall be in the end:
> My fragrance dwells in everything![22]

The oneness of the true master and God is a theme that emerges in mystic writings all over the world – a subject so misunderstood and difficult to comprehend by ordinary people that it has often cost the mystics their lives.

In a songpoem that narrates the ease of travelling within for the disciple who has done the inner work of self-transformation, Paltu refers to the extraordinary potential we each have for oneness with the divine. Speaking of our consciousness

or soul as the drop, and total consciousness
or the divine source as the ocean, he says that
when the soul has evolved to the ultimate level
of consciousness, God-realization,

> Who can separate them now?
> The Ocean has merged in the drop![23]

When the mystics speak of oneness and union,
they are not referring to the physical body, nor
even to the mind. They are talking about soul
consciousness, *surat*, which is the true identity or
pure essence of the mystic – and of everybody else.

The oneness they speak of is subtle and interior.
"Like fire in wood, fragrance in flowers – says the
slave Paltu, God lives like that in his devotees."[24]

From the exterior, the God-realized mystic
may appear to be a very ordinary human being –
perhaps a poor person with no education or social
standing, totally unknown and unrecognized,

working hard to earn a small income – a most brilliant light, nevertheless, shining through the darkness in their own particular corner of the world.

> Redness hidden in henna leaves,
> Butter and ghee in milk:
> That's the saints –
> Not one of them devoid of God.[25]

If the mystic is chosen by his own master to be the successor, as Paltu was, then he emerges, reluctantly, painfully, from the inconspicuous anonymity of being a disciple. He spends the rest of his life patiently explaining the teachings, encouraging disciples and initiating seekers. None of this is done for personal gain – everything is from obedience to his master. The aim: to help anybody in need, especially those who are seeking spiritual fulfilment and inner realization.

Anything is possible

Paltu is the mystic who said about the path: "In the game of love, whether heads or tails, it's God both ways: if I lose, I'm his – if I win, he's mine!"[26]

This saying and the songpoems of Paltu in *Dawn has come* remind us that the Naam bhakti path is a path of love – and in love, anything is possible. Or as Paltu puts it: "It's through the saints that everything comes about – whatever they wish is done!"[27]

What does the disciple contribute? As Paltu so humbly says: "There was this other Paltu. I was given the gift of devotion because they thought I was he. …Paltu, I am a no-good. God made a mistake. There was this other Paltu – he gave me devotion because he thought I was he."[28]

Paltu indicates that nobody deserves the gift of initiation – but once graced with that gift, then the disciple's contribution is to treasure it: to go on with the spiritual practice, without demands for results… simply because meditation is what pleases the master.

Speaking of the commitment needed for the long haul, Paltu says: "This business of yours will happen slowly, my friend – nothing is accomplished through hurry. The tree will fruit in its own good time, however much you may water it."[29]

Some mystics describe the mysterious inner power, God's Word or Name, as a current of pure love, linking each person to their spiritual origins. They say the purpose of the bhakti disciple's efforts and daily practice is to develop receptivity – to the master, the divine current, and everything they represent.

From that point of view, the evolving of consciousness and the extraordinary sights and sounds an advanced practitioner may experience are almost incidental – fabulous treasure, yes, but secondary to the main purpose, which is contacting and merging in the sound current.

It requires purity, humility, devotion and inward concentration – attributes that manifest as a result of the meditation practice itself. Ultimately, the process leads to the highly evolved spiritual state called "surrender" – and to the receptivity and spiritual maturity essential for the master's supreme gift: Love.

Paltu urges his disciples to focus, undistracted by the endless cravings of the mind: "This life is just four days long – do yourself a favour and meditate. Sacrifice body, mind and wealth at the feet of the saints. It's through them that everything comes about: whatever they wish is done. Yes, I tell you, Paltu, those who keep the company of the saints, even the Lord himself is in awe of them!"[30]

In some of the songpoems in this book, Paltu talks about experiences associated with the higher reaches of the inner path – those elusive spiritual heights that most of us do not experience, but which are, all the same, our birthright as human beings, say the mystics.

Is it easy to follow the inner way and claim that birthright? The average bhakti disciple might say *No*, but mystics like Paltu see the bigger picture. They know that if somebody is sincerely seeking an inner way and attempting to follow that way to its logical conclusion, they are almost there.

So close, say the mystics, that they already are what they wish to become: they just need to realize it – spiritually, within – even if it takes a lifetime of practice and seemingly fruitless effort. Says Paltu:

> It's inside your heart that you'll see –
> It will come into view,
> That light of the Lord.
>
> So where are you off to,
> In search of the light
> Of the Lord?[31]

"It's inside your heart that you'll see…"

Whatever our spiritual practice may be, the songpoems of Paltu in *Dawn has come* invite us to lean within and experience for ourselves the game of love he so joyfully plays.

Anthea Guinness
Phoenix, Arizona
1 August 2014

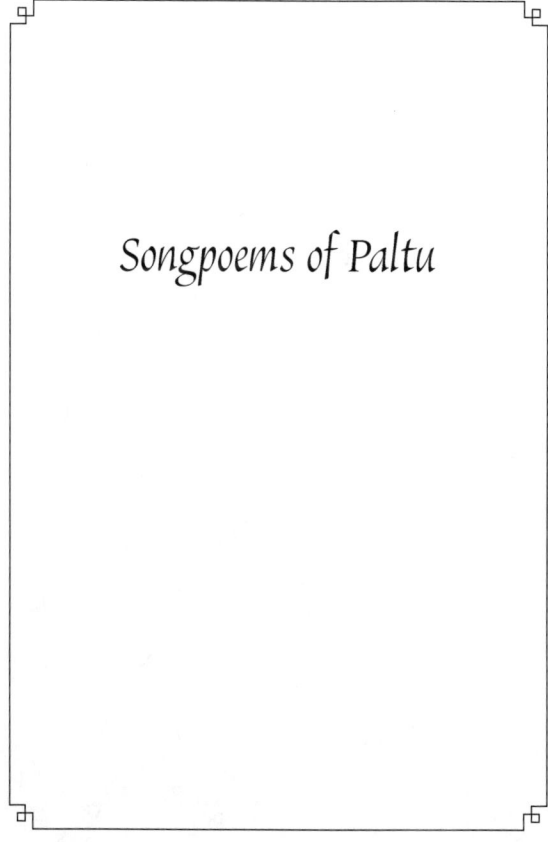

Songpoems of Paltu

$\mathcal{A}$nybody who comes
Into the company of a saint
Or listens to his discourses
Is ruined,
Absolutely spoilt,
Like cheap oil permeated
With the fragrance of flowers!

You can't avoid it –
In the company of a wise person
Foolishness goes, wisdom grows.
By the touch of a philosopher's stone
Base metal is ruined –

It loses all its characteristics
And becomes pure gold.

Look at the polluted streams
Flowing into the Ganges –
They're lost forever, inseparable
From that mother of rivers.
Even deadwood smells sweet
When stored near sandalwood.

This black crow Paltu
Has turned into a swan
And now all the crows are commiserating:

I warn you, friends –
Anybody who comes
Into the company of a saint
Is ruined forever!¹

❧

*F*inding God is easy –
It's finding a saint that's hard.

And unless you find a saint,
Says Paltu, God won't be enough:
You'll never be complete.²

❧

*T*he saint and God are one –
Time to recognize it!
Not a tad of difference
Between them.

Redness hidden in henna leaves,
Ghee in milk: set your heart
On this wisdom.

Fragrance in flowers, fire in wood –
It's exactly the same:
God inside the saints.

Says the slave Paltu,
Accept the truth, my friends:

God is in the saints
And the saints are in God!³

God puts on the form of a saint
And incarnates in the world:
He teaches the way of devotion
And sets people going on the path.

Whoever thinks God and God's people
Are two, says Paltu,
Will go straight to hell!⁴

$\mathcal{D}$iamonds don't grow in clusters,
Lions don't walk in herds:
Saints – they come in ones.

The rest are just beggars,
Eating away.[5]

❦

$\mathcal{A}$ tree doesn't grow fruit to feed itself,
A river doesn't drink its own water:

Saints take on a human body
For the sake of others.[6]

❦

Somebody who's beyond
Anger and lust,
Who isn't ruled
By hunger and thirst –

Yes, Paltu,
Darshan of a person like that
Will destroy your karmas![7]

I had a dream –
I saw it all while I was wide awake.
I saw it all: a river, wide and deep,
Flowing in three channels,
A city of crystal in the middle.

I saw a palace in complete darkness
Lit by an invisible flame.
A man was living there –
A being so brilliant
I became intoxicated, looking at him.

He began strumming a tune.
The first notes took me straight
To the One.
Listening to him play his melodies
Made me merge in the Sound.

Paltu, he was the Ancient One!
He had no form or colour or shape.
I was there in my dream.
I saw it all,
Wide awake.[8]

The melody from the skies of Trikuti –
Whoever brings that
Is my beloved master!
Yes, that is the divine master
And he is the one I will serve.

His state? Absorbed in Shabd.
Night and day detached:
He never feels hunger or thirst,
Cravings or desire.
He travels through the worlds
Of enlightenment
On an inturned breath.

He has gone beyond
Superconsciousness: purified,
He meditates in Tranquillity.
His meditation flows unbroken
Like the pour of oil –
He has mastered that purest
Of pure practices.

If I meet such a one, says Paltu,
I will sacrifice body and mind.
The melody from the skies of Trikuti –
Whoever brings that
Is my Beloved, the divine master![9]

The saints are lovers of Naam –
Naam is a lover of the saints!
Naam is in love with the saints,
And they alone can merge us in it.

They are the experts –
They show us the path to union.
Numerous people practise
Recitation and austerities
And go off on pilgrimages,
But without the intermediary,
The saint,
They never get to know the Name.

You can try a million methods
But you'll go on wandering
From birth to birth.
You need to go to the door
Of the saints –
Only then will you find
The home of Naam.

Paltu, Naam is beyond *praan,*
The subtle breath of life.
It was in the beginning,
It will be there in the end.
The saints are lovers of Naam,
And Naam, a lover of the saints![10]

When you meet satguru, the armourer,
That ancient stain will be removed.
That ancient stain, finally removed:
The mind has long been buried in rust.

Without the help of a perfect satguru
The stain will not go.
With the pumice of the path to union,
Keep scouring the sword!
It's only by using the rasp of attention
That you'll bring out the grain
Of the well-tempered sword.

Use Shabd as your grindstone,
Apply inner knowledge
As the abrasive. Scour away,
Using the practice you know
On this path towards union –
Then the stain on the mind will go.

Clean your sword, Paltu,
Hone it with inner detachment.
When you meet satguru, the armourer,
That ancient stain will be removed.[11]

*T*here's an upside-down well
In the skies within
Where a lamp is burning –
A lamp is burning
Without wick or oil.

All seasons of the year,
The twelve months through,
It goes on burning day and night.
If you meet a true master,
You'll see that lamp within.
It doesn't reveal itself
To the person who has no satguru.

A sound comes out of the flame
Of that lamp.
You'll hear it in deep meditation –
Otherwise you can't hear it.

Paltu, if anybody hears it,
They are most fortunate!
An upside-down well
In the skies within –
A lamp there, burning,
Burning within...[12]

*I*n the court of the Lord
There is only love and devotion.

Only love and devotion –
For devotion
Is what pleases the Lord.[13]

*I*t's inside your heart that you'll see –
It will come into view,
That light of the Lord.

So where are you off to,
In search of the light
Of the Lord?[14]

*I*f anybody wants the Name,
Heads up: the Name is nameless!

You can't write it or read it –
It's beyond marks and scratchings.

Its form? It is formless.
Like the wind, it leaves no tracks.

Yes, I tell you, Paltu,
With that mysterious inner vision
It's the saints who see the Name![15]

A flute is playing in the skies:
My mind is immersed, delighted!

My mind immersed, delighted –
I'm sitting here
In the eighth palace!
This is where the Shabd of "I am that"
Arises, and soul thrusts its way
Inside it.

Wave after wave of Sound emerging –
Colour, light, beauty: beyond
Anything one can say.

Moon and sun have set:
My bed is spread in Sushmana,
Hidden away beyond the eyes.
I escaped from this body,
Gave all my love to him alone.

I pierced through the Tenth Door –
The flame woke me up:
Beside myself with ecstasy!
Paltu, this meeting, this union,
Has the continuous unbroken
Pour of oil.

Dawn has come,
A flute is playing in the skies:
Mind – immersed, delighted!¹⁶

In the meeting of surat and Shabd
I've become filled with bliss!

Filled with bliss –
Water merged in water.¹⁷

The house of the Beloved is far away.
One in a million will reach it.

One in a million –
The ones who get there are perfect jogis:
They've renounced the world,
Burnt lust to ashes,
But right in their own home indulge
In the bliss of Sound.

They die while living
And once dead, get up alive.
If there's somebody who can do all this,
They'll be prepared to do the rest.

You are torn to shreds,
Blown away in the wind.
No food... clothing... water...
You have to let go
Of everything: robbed empty,
Laughed at, abandoned.

Someone who lasts out unmoving
Can be called a lover.
The house of the Beloved is far away.
It's somebody like that
    who will reach it.[18]

I love him.
Mother, I love him!
Do you understand?
He has taken my heart.
I cannot survive
Unless I see this Lord of mine.

My life is worthless –
Pennies to throw as an offering:
Let him have all of them!
I'm sick. I'm dying.

But there is one cure:
If I could find, merge,
With my dearly Beloved.

Look at this love he's entangled me in!
Somehow he's filled my breast
With remembrance of his names.
I fall down unconscious.
Fear of what people think?
That ran away long ago.

Who can understand, Paltu,
Except my Physician, my satguru!
I love him, mother. I love him.
He has taken my heart.
I cannot survive![19]

*M*y whole body is on fire!
My Beloved's sweet voice
Started the blaze.
His sweet voice, I heard it –
Went mad.

The song of "I am that"
Rings out from the depths
Of the revolving cave.
I saw my Beloved there –
His beautiful face!
Merged in that form.

Ever since our union
We've never been apart.
This love of ours goes back
Beyond beginnings:
I realize it now.

A flame found the Flame
And merged in it.
Soul wedded,
Became one.
Forever.

The moment I heard the Sound, Paltu,
He tore away my veil.

Beloved – your face, your voice –
You've set my whole body on fire![20]

❧

*H*e destroyed caste, class, race, name –
He set me going With the essence of
   devotion.

In the garden of Guru Gobind,
Paltu blossomed
Like a flower.[21]

❧

*S*o tender, soft –
No one but the saints is like that!
You can't hold a candle to them –
They are kind and compassionate
To all without exception.

Friend or foe? He treats them alike.
Good fortune or bad? The same.
Gentle as flowers, he doesn't want
To see others' faults even in a dream.

He looks on all with affection,
For he drinks his fill of love's nectar
Like we drink sugarcane juice!

Friendly, smiling, his sweet words
And a voice that catches your heart
Thrill people with delight,
Leaving them overjoyed
As he passes, serene,
His glance showering jewels
Of grace and good fortune.

Paltu, whatever one might say to them,
They're not disturbed even for a second.
So tender, soft –
No one but the saints is like that!²²

I was in the beginning,
I shall be in the end:
My fragrance dwells in everything.
I am the one who lives in everything –
Nothing else besides that.

The divine powers –
Brahma, Vishnu, Mahesh –
Are all forms of me:
I am the one who sustains,
I am the one who destroys.

I am the one within each and every body,
Yet I remain apart from all.

Parbrahm and the Lord of Creation
Are just particles of me,
Doing what I say.

The Shabd of "I am that" is me.
From this emerges the flame
In the darkness of Sunn, the Void.

Paltu, because of this human form
He is the Lord, I am his slave.
I was in the beginning,
I shall be in the end:
My fragrance dwells in everything![23]

An ascetic was wandering
Through the town,
Lost in himself, carefree.
He was rising up within,
Going from palace to palace,
Mad with ecstasy.

He didn't eat, didn't drink, didn't beg.
He didn't speak, didn't stumble.
But how he danced!
Danced without dancing
To a melody no one played.

He found nectar dripping everywhere
In the house of happiness –

Drank from a curving tube.
Whenever you see him
He's full to the brim with love,
Repeating the unrepeatable Name
That has no rosary.

This wandering ascetic sounded a horn
In the cave of Trikuti's sky.
He stayed awake
In the realm of wakefulness,
Sat in meditation
At the confluence of three rivers,
A lover in love
With the Lord beyond Lords.

He took a vow of silence
When he sat in the Void
But played the music
Of the unstruck drum.
By the time he entered
The realm of Turiya
He could hardly speak for tears of joy.

And then he began to sing a song,
His voice reverberating – loud, long.
Our jogi became the Sound:
Merged, one Shabd to another.
The granite gates in the skies of Trikuti
Crumbled to dust!

Says the slave Paltu,
Who can separate them now?
The Ocean has merged
In the drop![24]

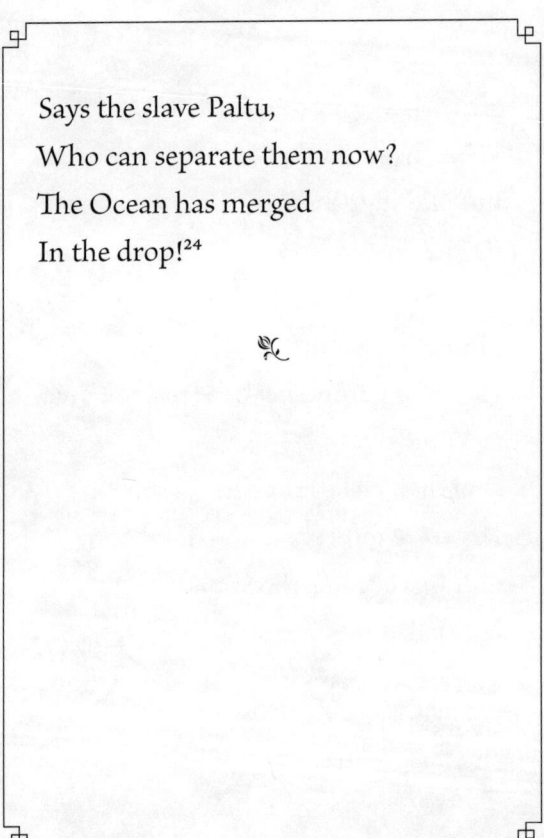

There was this other Paltu.
I was given the gift of devotion
Because they thought I was he.
I caught the Name
He was supposed to get –
Paltu's devotion was given to me.

I found it lying there:
Somebody had dropped
This incredible wealth.
I picked it up casually,
Closed my hands over it,
Hid it away.

It was fated otherwise
But somehow
It got mixed in with my karmas.
I was the only one who knew –
Nobody else had any idea.

Eventually they found out.
They thought about it
But didn't take it back.
That's the way of the rich –
If they make a blunder
They can afford to let it go.

Paltu, I am a no-good.
God made a mistake.
There was this other Paltu –
He gave me devotion
Because he thought I was he.[25]

EXPLORATIONS

GLOSSARY

alive According to the bhakti mystics, really being alive means not being subject to the laws of karma and transmigration; instead, one becomes fully alive in oneness with Life – the supreme Being.

armourer The crafting of personal armour and weaponry is one of the ancient trades worldwide; an armourer would know how to make, mend and maintain arms in excellent condition. Satguru as armourer provides the disciple with everything he/she needs for carrying out the unrelenting inner struggle against the mind, not least the method for cleansing, uplifting and strengthening the mind itself to combat the tendencies of the lower mind.

awake Being in a state of realization or awakened **consciousness**; being "asleep" often refers

to the unrealized state where the reactive mind
governs one's thoughts, feelings and behaviour.

Beloved   The master, the Friend, the Friend of
God, the Lord, the Shabd or Shabd master.

bhakti   Devotion. Bhakti disciple, bhakti mystic,
bhakti tradition: *see* **Naam bhakti tradition**

consciousness   In the bhakti understanding,
soul is consciousness – a drop of the ocean of
consciousness, which is God. At the ordinary
level of human experience, our consciousness
is shrouded; we perceive very little beyond
the physical surface. At the stage of full con-
sciousness or realization, soul is free from its
coverings (physical and mental) and attains to
total consciousness (also called Shabd, Naam,
Tao, Spirit). Mystics like Kabir, Nanak, Paltu,
Tulsi and Shiv Dayal Singh use a special word
for consciousness: *surat*, synonymous with
attention; the soul's faculty of hearing; the soul.

crow, swan   Unrealized soul contrasted with soul
liberated from body and mind – "pure soul".

curving tube   *bank naal*: Subtle passageway within.

darshan   Seeing, beholding, gazing: Looking at the master, inside oneself or outside, with attention so absorbed in the master that one is aware of nothing else.

Daswaa Dwaar   *See* **Tenth Door**

dawn   Spiritual enlightenment, the dawning of inner light and understanding, the experience of light and spiritual realization within.

death   *See* **dying while living**

devotee   God-realized **mystic**.

devotion, *bhakti*   In the **Naam bhakti** mystic tradition, devotion refers to doing the inner meditation practice taught by the teacher. According to mystics like Kabir and Paltu, the particular focus of the practice is inner attuning and oneness in the divine power, the Word or Name (*shabd* or *naam*) – also called Spirit, Kalma, the Great Mystery, Tao – through love, humility, séva (service) and meditation.

Sometimes "the gift of devotion" refers to *naam daan*, the gift of initiation.

door of the saints The company of the true master, his talks (satsang), initiation and the eye centre are the door that leads within.

dying while living Mystics describe the withdrawal of consciousness from the body in focused meditation as "dying while living" or "dying before death" – a prelude to fully contacting the life current of Shabd within and waking up to enlightenment and everlasting life.

eighth palace May refer to the supreme level of consciousness, *anaami* or Nameless.

eye centre Focal point in the forehead for meditation, also referred to as "beyond the eyes", the heart, the sesame seed.

on fire Divine love.

flame Inner light.

flute Inner sound associated with the level of self-realization. See **I am that**

Friend The **master**, the **Beloved**.

God-realization   Merging or oneness with the
supreme level of consciousness.

granite gates in the skies of Trikuti   The
threshold to the purely spiritual levels of
consciousness at the peak of the mind's realm.

haq   Arabic word for "truth": often used by
Sufis in repeated recitations (zikr). For mystics,
the hearing of the sound *haq* refers to an
inner experience, not the outer repetition of
a spoken word; it is the sound of Truth itself
resounding – Kalma, Ism-i Aazam or Shabd
at the supreme level of consciousness where
twoness or duality has been transcended (soul
has separated from mind) and soul and Spirit
"become One".

heart   *See* **eye centre**

home   The Beloved coming to one's home: the
manifesting of the Shabd master within.

home or house of the Beloved, home of Naam
The supreme level of consciousness, God-
realization. This is the true home of the saints

or fully realized mystics; it is the origins and
therefore the real home of every soul.

house of happiness, *sukhman ké ghar* See
Sushmana

I am that *so aham* in Sanskrit: The triumphant
declaration of the soul when it reaches the stage
of self-realization, for the first time seeing
itself as pure soul and contemplating the final
stage before it: God-realization. **Shabd of
"I am that":** the Shabd at the penultimate level
of consciousness.

Ingala and Pingala *eeRa* and *pingala*. See
Sushmana

invisible *gaib*: Not visible to the physical eyes;
a word Paltu uses for inner subtle perception.

jogi Yogi. Occasionally used as affectionate term
for the master or disciples. Paltu sometimes
contrasts the path of the yogis (ascetic practices,
outer renunciation of the world, restraint,
self-control, suppression; drinking hemp as
a way to get high) with the inner practice of

a bhakti disciple ("indulging" in the bliss of Sound, "drinking" elixir inside, "high" on love intoxication; inner renunciation or natural detachment through attachment to Shabd; not governed by desire – for food, water, or anything else).

karma Lit. action: The universal law of cause and effect; reaping what we have sown, both negative and positive. The karmic law works in tandem with the law of transmigration (repeatedly taking birth in any of numerous life forms), both laws together keeping the soul imprisoned in an unending series of lifetimes in the lower regions – the physical, astral and causal worlds – until the soul's ever-growing karmic debt has been fully accounted for, leading to the liberation of the soul. Desires and actions in previous lives influence our present life; desires and actions in the present influence our future destiny. Bhakti mystics take the laws of karma and transmigration for granted but do not require their students to believe in them; they say that one automatically sees these laws at work in all their complexity at higher levels of realization.

lamp, light Shabd manifests inside as sound, which projects light. The light is attractive and enables the individual to see the onward path; the sound gives a sense of direction.

the Lord of Creation A reference to the universal mind, Brahm or Kaal.

the Lord beyond Lords Paarbrahm, lit. beyond Brahm or universal mind.

love God is love; the goal or destination of the Naam bhakti path is to become more and more attuned to the pure spiritual frequency of divine love, the Shabd or Naam, and merge in it at the highest levels of consciousness. Soul (initiate) and Shabd (master) are often described by mystics as lover/beloved, bride/groom, wife/husband; the non-physical union or consummation of their "marriage" (initiation) takes place when the drop (soul) ultimately merges in the wave of Shabd (the master), which leads to their oneness in the ocean of Shabd (God-realization) – completing the soul's return to its original state of love and oneness in God, the source.

master In the Naam bhakti tradition, the mystic teacher is appointed by his own teacher before his death to pass on the spiritual practice to others and guide them to the highest levels of consciousness – self-realization and God-realization. The real form of such a teacher is Shabd or Spirit, in which form he accompanies his disciples everywhere, at all times, during life and after death. The bhakti master is a living master; he is spiritually responsible only for disciples he accepts for initiation during his physical lifetime.

meditation A practice of inner focusing. Bhakti mystics speak of three aspects of meditation, done under the supervision of a master: *simran* or repetition, *dhyaan* or contemplation, *dhun* or listening to the inner sound.

melody *See* **Shabd**

merge The bhakti practice is about merging surat (consciousness, soul) in Shabd (Word, Sound) at higher and higher frequencies or levels of consciousness, sometimes expressed as merging "in Shabd after Shabd" or "merged, one Shabd to another".

mind Bhakti mystics differentiate body *(tan)*, mind *(man)*, and soul *(rooh* or *aatma)* or consciousness *(surat)*. Mind is inanimate – a tool, not an entity – powered and enlivened by the energy of soul; unenlightened mind is often identified with ego, I-ness, self.

moon and sun Significant inner constellations on the initial stage of the evolution of consciousness. Once this stage has been passed, "moon and sun have set", is how Paltu puts it.

mystic Generally speaking, a mystic is somebody who carries out an inner spiritual practice with the goal of realizing the inner mysteries. Mystics in different traditions adopt a wide range of methods and techniques to achieve their particular goals. In the Naam bhakti tradition, the goal is self-realization and God-realization; the mystic (*sant*, saint) is a disciple who has achieved it. Like other disciples, he/she does the meditation practice taught by the master and lives the way of life he recommends. Such disciples have gone beyond the numerous subtle levels of consciousness associated with the mind and have merged in the oneness of spiritual realization at the highest levels of consciousness. While there may be several such bhakti mystics or fully realized disciples living unobtrusively here and there, the master is the one who has been appointed by his predecessor during his lifetime to carry on the onerous work of initiating seekers and providing spiritual guidance.

Naam, Name, the Name of God   The divine power that is one with God and that creates and sustains the universe; audible and visible within us as sound and light. It is not a written or spoken word, so it is sometimes called "the nameless Name". Also referred to by mystics as Spirit, Word (*shabd, kalma, logos*), Music, Sound, Truth, Tao, Secret, Sama', Voice, Way – among many other terms.

Naam bhakti tradition   Various independent lines of mystics in India, traceable from at least the 1100s to present time (including Hindu, Muslim and Sikh teachers), who practise and teach the way of attuning and then merging individual consciousness (*surat*) in the divine power known as the Name (*naam*), the Word (*shabd, kalma*).

name(s), repeating the name(s)   *See* **simran**

ocean of existence   *bhav saagar:* The bhakti mystics commonly refer to the worlds ruled by mind, karma and transmigration as the ocean of existence; crossing safely by means of the divine current of Shabd or Naam to the other side of that vast realm of consciousness means true freedom or spiritual liberation.

palace   Sometimes a general reference to inner levels of consciousness, as in "many mansions" and "going from palace to palace" within.

Parbrahm   *See* **Lord beyond Lords**

play, pleasure   The ecstasy of oneness with the Beloved (the Shabd or formless Shabd form of the master) at high levels of consciousness.

radiant form   The astral or inner light form of the teacher. The radiant form is projected within the disciple by the teacher from Shabd; it is visible beyond the eye centre.

remembrance of his names   Simran, zikr.

revolving cave   *bha~war gupha*: associated with self-realization. *See also* **I am that**

sacrifice   When the mystics speak of sacrificing body, mind and wealth to the master, they are not talking literally about external offerings, but rather the numerous daily sacrifices the disciple has to make on the path – including the discipline of living a lifestyle that excludes alcohol, hallucinogenic drugs, animal foods (meat, fish, eggs) and casual sex, and that includes the challenge to be a kind, non-violent, decent human being, quietly being of service to those in need and generally attempting to curb the ego by focusing the mind when free on inner remembrance (simran, Shabd).

saint, *sant*   True master; fully realized **mystic**.

satguru   True master. *See also* **master**, **mystic**

Shabd   Lit. word, sound: The divine energy that creates and sustains the universe, audible and visible within as sound and light; also referred to as Naam, the Name. Shabd form of the master: a formless form; sometimes refers to the astral or **radiant form**.

simran   Remembrance, repetition: Mental repetition of sacred names given by the spiritual teacher to initiates, sometimes referred to as continuous interior prayer. In the bhakti

tradition, simran or silent zikr is for focusing
the mind within in order to hear the Shabd
and realize the mysterious power of the Name.

songpoems *shabds, kunᴅlis:* Most compositions
of pre-twentieth century bhakti mystics were
in the form of lyrics – easy for non-readers
to memorize, sing and recite, and written in
simple language anybody could understand.

Sound Shabd, the Word.

superconsciousness *See* **Turiya**

surat A term used in the Naam bhakti tradition
to mean **consciousness**, soul.

Surat Shabd The path that is practised and
taught by the Naam bhakti mystics: the
merging of surat (consciousness) in Shabd
(Word, Sound). Also called Surat Shabd
Yoga – union, *yog,* of consciousness in Shabd.
See also **Naam bhakti tradition**

Sushmana, Sushumna, Sukhmana, Sukhman
(-*u*- as in push) In bhakti writings, refers to the

central passageway beyond the eye centre, with two other passages, *eeʀa* and *pingala,* on the left and right; the same terminology is used in the yogic tradition, but it refers to three currents of energy associated with the spine.

swan "Pure soul" – individual consciousness liberated from body and mind.

Tenth Door The eye centre is referred to as "the tenth" in bhakti writings (the other nine doors being the external outlets of the body: eyes, nose, etc.); the advanced level of consciousness beyond the higher mind (Trikuti) is called the Tenth Door, *daswaa~ dwaar.*

Tranquillity *sahaj*: natural, inherent, easy, spontaneous, calm, equipoised; used in mystic writings for the soul's "natural state" when it returns to the level of consciousness known as God-realization; beyond **Turiya.**

Trikuti Level of consciousness associated with the higher mind.

Truth *See* **Naam**

Turiya   Blissful state of superconsciousness; fourth state of consciousness, beyond the waking, sleeping and unconscious states.

union   *jog* or *yog(a):* The goal of the Naam bhakti path is the merging of consciousness (surat) in the ocean of total consciousness (Shabd) at the highest level (God-realization). The union the mystics refer to is not physical, mental or intellectual, but an advanced level of awakening or oneness of soul in the divine.

unstruck drum   *See* **Shabd**

vision, mysterious inner vision   *gaib drish*ᴛɪ: lit. invisible seeing; spiritual power to see inside.

the Void   Sunn, a spiritual level of consciousness beyond or devoid of mind.

well   The "upside-down well" refers to the portion of the head above the eyes, the dome of the head being the bottom of the well. This is where the inner light and sound manifest and the entire journey of consciousness unfolds.

Word   One of the terms commonly used in sacred traditions to refer to the creative power of God, manifest within as sound and light: viz. Kalma (Sufi tradition), Logos (Greek mystic tradition), **Shabd** (bhakti tradition).

PALTU

Very little is known about Paltu, except what can be gleaned from his writings and the writings of his contemporaries.

Paltu came from a village near Ayodhya in Uttar Pradesh. He lived during the reign of Shaah Aalam, the Moghul emperor in Delhi – but there were two Shah Alams in the 1700s, with no indication which one was Paltu's contemporary. Perhaps both were, making Paltu's dates approximately 1710–1780. It is equally plausible, however, that Paltu was born earlier than that, in the late 1600s – or later, with his lifespan overlapping the early 1800s.

In his teenage years, Paltu set out in search of a true master. He eventually came to Gobind, the living master in the line of Bhikh (*bheekh*)

of Saharanpur, U.P. (different from the Sikh
teacher, Gobind Singh of Punjab, 1666–1708).

> Broke my karmic chains,
> Brought an end to my wandering –
> That is Gobind!
> This is what happens
> When you meet Gobind –
> He spits on the world
> Of coming-and-going![1]

Paltu was exceptional as a disciple – full of
love and devotion for his master, which he quietly
channelled into meditation. This one-pointed
focus led to meeting the Shabd master within:

> This slave Paltu's Gobind Sahib
> Came to meet me
> In the lane of love.[2]

In a songpoem where Paltu speaks as soul, he says she is completely love intoxicated – daughter of her kingly father, "Gobind the Blissful"!

> Dear friend, Paltu has gone mad
> With love intoxication!
> I am a princess,
> Beloved daughter of my King,
> Gobind the Blissful.[3]

Elsewhere, Paltu mentions the type of worship he offers to his master Gobind – inside. His purely spiritual adoration is expressed at the feet of the Shabd master within, through his attunement to the inner sound and light of Shabd:

> All hail to Guru Gobind –
> All hail, all hail!
> I worship you with sound and light!

Seeing your feet inside,
Tasting that lotus nectar within,
Millions of the fallen
Have been ferried across.[4]

Young Paltu's transformation and inner realization were so exceptional that his master one day exclaimed, *Yé to palaт gayaa!* – "This one has really transformed" – and from that time on his name became *palтoo,* the transformed one. His birth name is not known.

Paltu's ancestral trade was shopkeeping. He probably had a tiny grocery shop in the market, selling lentils, flour, rice, salt and other everyday vegetarian food staples, supporting his wife and their children.

Paltu settled in Ayodhya on the orders of his master, who also told him to give satsang (talks) on the inner path of Shabd and Naam, and to initiate sincere seekers into the mystic way.

In one of his songpoems, Paltu describes this work as a master in terms of shopkeeping. He says his master has elevated him to the royal position of "God's storekeeper" (spiritual teacher) and his business is no longer in the marketplace but in the spiritual realms, where he is kept busy "selling pearls" to customers (sharing the mystic teachings and initiation at no charge with sincere seekers):

> Who will sell my goods now?
> Who will sell my goods?
> My stores are in Trikuti,
> My seat in Sukhman passage,
> My warehouse in Daswaa Dwaar,
> Governed by an eternal being.

Ingala and Pingala, passageways
To left and right, are the two pans
Of the balance, strung
With the light of consciousness;
True Word, the balance beam I'm holding
As I weigh out panfuls of pearls.

The sun and moon are both caretakers,
Guarding this little pile of the Essence!
Turiya fills my display
And keeps me busy selling –
Such is the eminence I've attained.

My master showered his grace
And I was elevated to be
God's storekeeper.
In Paltu's house a drum is beating –
And his trade grows more and more!⁵

Paltu's fame as a spiritual teacher began to spread. The mystic teachings he shared were simple and were offered freely to everybody, regardless of gender, religion, race or social standing.

Like all mystics, Paltu emphasized that God is within and can only be attained within. He therefore taught that external worship of any kind is worthless in that it has no spiritual benefit – including rites and rituals, pilgrimages and fasting, rote prayers, singing, recitation of scriptures, and ritual visits to places of worship. Instead, he offered to teach people how to meditate quietly in their own homes.

Their income threatened by Paltu's growing influence, the priests, pundits and magistrates in Ayodhya's Hindu temples and Muslim mosques made a plan to end Paltu's life. Barring the door of his hut one night, they burned him alive.

It seems Paltu did nothing to save himself. He must have known that his time had come. Like mystics before and since, he surrendered to the

will of the Lord without complaint, knowing
beforehand exactly what was to come.

Paltu's beautiful songpoems and mystic teachings
lived on, handed down orally for generations until
the songpoems were published in book form in
the early 1900s by Belvedere press.

His message – discussed by spiritual teachers
from the 1800s on – and his songpoems, sung to a
melody used only for Paltu, continue to electrify
satsang audiences all over India to this day.

PALTU BOOKS

In the late 1800s the founder of Belvedere Printing Works, Allahabad, and his associates – themselves disciples of a bhakti teacher – travelled all over north and west India, copying manuscripts and writing down oral traditions of Kabir, Mira, Paltu and other bhakti mystics.

These unique recordings were published by Belvedere from about 1902 on as a series of small volumes – years before standard editions of bhakti compositions became generally available.

The Belvedere edition of Paltu in Hindi, *Paltu Sahib ki shabdavali* in 3 volumes, is the standard text for Paltu's writings.

The most extensive English translation of Paltu is Isaac Ezekiel's groundbreaking work, *Saint Paltu: his life and teachings* (1978). The Salt River *Inner way* anthology also includes songpoems by Paltu.

INDEX OF SONGPOEMS

Index of songpoems

ENDNOTES

The Belvedere edition of Paltu is the Hindi source for all the selections in this book: *Paltu Sahib ki shabdavali* (Allahabad: Belvedere Printing Works), 3 vols.

Introduction

1. Commons. Cf. Sawan Singh, *"yaa bheekh!"* English version by Anthea Guinness. Punjabi source: *Parmaarthi saakhiyaa~* (RSSB, 1964). For a collection of mystic stories told by Sawan Singh, see *Tales of the mystic East* (RSSB).
2. Bhikh *(bheekh)* of Saharanpur in the later 1500s is different from the mystic Bhikha *(bhikkha)* of Punjab, a Hindu devotee of the master Amar Das (lineage of Nanak, mid-1500s). Gobind of Uttar Pradesh, the master of Paltu, is not the same teacher as Gobind Singh of Punjab (lineage of Nanak, late 1600s).
3. Isaac A. Ezekiel, *Saint Paltu* (RSSB, 1978). See also the *Inner way* anthology (SRP, 2013), which highlights the writings of the Naam bhakti mystics, including

songpoems by Paltu. To date, several hundred Paltu compositions remain untranslated into English.

4. Paltu: *"bhav sindhu ké paar jo chaahiyé"* (2:1 *rékhta*).

5. Paltu: *"sabad chhuʀaavai raaj ko"* (1:88 *kunɒli*), excerpts.

6. Paltu: *"naam ké ré partaap sé"* (1:16 *kunɒli*), excerpts.

7. Paltu: *"sant sanéhi naam hai"* (1:14 *kunɒli*), *Dawn* 10, excerpt.

8. Paltu: *"koʈin jug parlay ga'ee"* (1:177 *kunɒli*).

9. Paltu: *"hawa ka~hai khaamos karai"* (2:44 *jhoolna*). This little verse is packed with Sufi (Arabic) terms, perhaps written in particular for Muslim seekers.

10. Examples of other selections in this book that refer to the sound and light of Shabd or Naam: *Dawn* 8, 9, 12, 14, 16, 18, 20, 24.

11. Paltu: *"phirai ik jogi nagar bhulaana"* (3:129 *shabd*), *Dawn* 24, excerpt.

12. Paltu: *"dhun aanai jo gagan ki"* (1:5 *kunɒli*), *Dawn* 9, excerpt. Paltu uses *gurudév* here to refer to the master of Shabd, a term for master that expresses affection and respect as well as literally meaning "divine" (*dév*) master; perhaps he is deliberately emphasizing that the true Shabd master is not an ordinary teacher (*guru*), but a God-realized "divine" master, a *guru-dév*.

13. Paltu: *"kya sovai too baavari"* (1:41 *kunɒli*), excerpts.

14. Paltu: *"raam ka milana sahaj hai"* (3:73 *saakhi*), *Dawn* 2.

15. A much-quoted saying in the West: "When the *chéla* (disciple) is ready, the guru appears."

16. Paltu: *"jo jo ga satsang mé~"* (1:85 *kunɒli*), *Dawn* 1, excerpts.

17. Paltu: *"vriccha pharai na aap ko"* (3:111 *saakhi*), *Dawn* 6.

18. Paltu: *"seetal chandan chandrama"* (1:23 *kunɒli*), excerpt, reprinted with permission from *The inner way* 81 (Salt River Publishing, 2013).

19. Paltu: *"seetal chandan chandrama"* (1:23 *kunɒli*), excerpt, from *The inner way* 81 (Salt River Publishing, 2013).

20. Paltu: *"sant baraabar komal"* (1:24 *kunɒli*), *Dawn* 22, excerpt.

21. Paltu: *"sant baraabar komal"* (1:24 *kunɒli*), *Dawn* 22, excerpt.

22. Paltu: *"aadi ant ham hee~ rahé"* (1:178 *kunɒli*), *Dawn* 23, excerpts. See endnote 23, Sayings.

23. Paltu: *"phirai ik jogi nagar bhulaana"* (3:129 *shabd*), excerpt, *Dawn* 24.

24. Paltu: *"jaisé kaaᴛh mé~ agin hai"* (3:49 *saakhi*). An interesting ambiguity in the final line: it could be translated "God lives in his devotees – like that is the slave Paltu."

25. Paltu: *"mi~hdi mé~ laali rahai"* (3:50 *saakhi*). *laali* (first line) means redness, but it also connotes the Beloved.

26. Paltu: *"palᴛoo baaji laa'ihau~"* (3:28 *saakhi*).
27. Paltu: *"jeevan hai din chaar"* (2:8 *aril*), excerpt.
28. Paltu: *"doosar palᴛoo ik raha"* (1:164 *kunᴅli*), excerpt, *Dawn* 25.
29. Paltu: *"kaaraj dheeré hot hai"* (3:110 *saakhi*). *dheeré* (slowly) has the same root as *dheer* (patience) and *adheer* (impatience, hurry), juxtaposed by Paltu in the same line.
30. Paltu: *"jeevan hai din chaar"* (2:8 *aril*), excerpt.
31. Paltu: *"dil mé~ aavai hai nazar"* (1:94 *kunᴅli*), excerpt, *Dawn* 14.

Songpoems

1. Paltu: *"jo jo ga satsang mé~"* (1:85 *kunᴅli*).
2. Paltu: *"raam ka milana sahaj hai"* (3:73 *saakhi*).
3. Paltu: *"sant au raam ko ék kai jaaniyé"* (2:17 *rékhta*).
4. Paltu: *"hari harijan ko du'i kahai"* (1:32 *kunᴅli*), excerpt. The dominant line that echoes and re-echoes (first, second and last lines) is "Whoever says God and God's people are two will go straight to hell" – the impact intensified by the sounds, rhythm and deliberate word-plays: *hari harijan* (God; God's people) and *nar narak* (person; hell): *"hari harijan ko du'i kahai, so nar narakai jaay"*.
5. Paltu: *"nahi~ heera boran chalai"* (3:159 *saakhi*).

6. Paltu: *"vriccha pharai na aap ko"* (3:111 *saakhi*).
7. Paltu: *"kaam krodh jin ké nahee~"* (3:58 *saakhi*).
8. Paltu: *"jaagat mé~ ék soopana"* (1:175 *kunᴅli*).
9. Paltu: *"dhun aanai jo gagan ki"* (1:5 *kunᴅli*). See endnote 12, Introduction.
10. Paltu: *"sant sanéhi naam hai"* (1:14 *kunᴅli*).
11. Paltu: *"satguru sikaleegar milai~"* (1:2 *kunᴅli*).
12. Paltu: *"ulᴛa koowaa gagan mé~"* (1:169 *kunᴅli*).
13. Paltu: *"saahib ké darbaar mé~"* (1:218 *kunᴅli*), excerpt.
14. Paltu: *"dil mé~ aavai hai nazar"* (1:94 *kunᴅli*), excerpt.
15. Paltu: *"jo ko'i chaahai naam"* (2:2 *aril*).
16. Paltu: *"ba~si baaji gagan mé~"* (1:170 *kunᴅli*).
17. Paltu: *"surat shabd ké milan mé~"* (1:89 *kunᴅli*), excerpt.
18. Paltu: *"aasik ka ghar door hai"* (1:72 *kunᴅli*).
19. Paltu: *"amma méra dil laga"* (1:63 *kunᴅli*).
20. Paltu: *"méré tan tan lag ga'i"* (1:59 *kunᴅli*).
21. Paltu: *"chaari baran ko méᴛi kai"* (3:143 *saakhi*).
22. Paltu: *"sant baraabar komal"* (1:24 *kunᴅli*).
23. Paltu: *"aadi ant ham hee~ rahé"* (1:178 *kunᴅli*). *baas* in line 1 has two meanings (fragrance, trace, F.; dwelling, M.): while the line literally means "I live in everything" (*sab mé~ méro baas*), the echo of "fragrance" in *baas* is an unconscious association in Hindi; it adds poetic intensity to the line and blends with the literal meaning, so "fragrance" has been included in this English version.

24. Paltu: *"phirai ik jogi nagar bhulaana"* (3:129 *shabd*), reprinted with permission from *The inner way* 158 (Salt River Publishing, 2013).

25. Paltu: *"doosar palᴛu ik raha"* (1:164 *kunᴅli*), reprinted with permission from *The inner way* 57 (Salt River Publishing, 2013). Cf. earlier version in *Saint Paltu* (ʀssʙ, 1999), p.194.

Paltu

1. Paltu: *"karam janéoo toʀi kai"* (3:26 *saakhi*).

2. Paltu: *"palᴛoodaas ké gobind saahib"* (3:57 *shabd*), excerpt.

3. Paltu: *"sakhi palᴛoo almast diwaani"* (3:127 *shabd*), excerpt. Here Paltu deliberately speaks as though he were a girl talking with her *priya-sakhi* or girlfriend, her confidante, as one soul to another.

4. Paltu: *"jai jai jai guroo gobind"* (3:12 *shabd*), excerpt. Paltu speaks here of *aarti*, a traditional Hindu ceremony involving light and sound. Like Shiv Dayal Singh and other bhakti mystics, Paltu uses the term *aarti* to refer to an inner or mystic experience of adoration, thanksgiving and spiritual merging, resonant with inner light and sound.

5. Paltu: *"kaun karai baniyaa'i ab moré"* (3:81 *shabd*).

SPIRITUAL RESEARCH

Mystic writings may inspire one with a desire to have a spiritual practice and a genuine spiritual guide. Several questions naturally arise: Is every spiritual teacher a true master? Is every mystic capable of being an inner guide? Is every "mystic practice" part of the true way? Can one follow a spiritual path on one's own, without an expert guide?

We are graced with inquiring minds and a need to be intellectually satisfied. There is no reason to settle for anything less. The following points, culled from the talks and writings of the mystics, may help as reminders and touchstones at any time in our life.

True masters always live the path they teach. They do not claim that the path they follow is the only way and they encourage seekers to research thoroughly before making a commitment. They do not sit in judgement on any other teacher or any other teaching. They seek no mundane advantage from their work. For them, the sharing of truth is not a commercial transaction; they do not charge money, whether for giving talks or for passing on the inner practice.

True masters are willing to answer a seeker's questions but make no attempt to persuade, reminding seekers that conviction must come from within, not through words or emotions. They behave in private and in public with complete integrity. They use donations in the service of others, providing for their own needs from their own family income.

Do such teachers exist? Yes. But the bottom line is that most of us are not evolved enough to differentiate a true master from a teacher of lesser spiritual standing. How can a child in kindergarten have any idea of the academic level attained by her teacher! When in doubt, one needs to go on looking. Sincerity, longing, searching – these are what count. As a seeker, it is entirely appropriate to ask questions about the practice and the path one is interested in, to air one's doubts and to study carefully any books about the path.

A contemporary mystic says: If you spend your whole life in spiritual research, it is not time wasted, it is time gained. When your intellect is satisfied, you will move forward without hesitation on your spiritual journey.

ACKNOWLEDGEMENTS

As always, I feel deep gratitude for supportive friends, family, teachers and colleagues. It is a pleasure to acknowledge a few by name; I thank also the ones not named here – particularly the colleagues who made allowances for growing pains and worked with me so tolerantly throughout my years in India.

Much appreciation to my sister Chloe Wordsworth, whose periodic reminders about small books ultimately set in motion this series of little books on the mystics – and for her helpful suggestions.

To Carol White, designer of books, for her willingness to work with her authors – open to their requests and ideas, and creative in her solutions.

Acknowledgements

To Berkeley Digby for his careful reading of the introduction and his insightful suggestions. To Cindy Rawlinson, Connie Rawlinson, Ronald Youlton and Lindis Guinness for their warm response and helpful feedback.

To Renu Bhagat, for happily addressing the odd Hindi question, and to another colleague for tracking down some elusive Hindi verses.

Special thanks to VK Sethi, author of *Kabir, the weaver of God's Name* and *Mira, the divine lover.* Colleague, mentor, friend, he years ago shared his love for Kabir and filled my mind with images of India's traditions – secular, literary and spiritual – that I've been drawing on ever since.

My thanks to the late Isaac A. Ezekiel for *Saint Paltu: his life and teachings* (RSSB, 1978) – the only book of Paltu translations in English that I have come across. It was very helpful while I studied Paltu's songpoems in Hindi and then translated them into English.

Profound gratitude for my family! My parents, John and Karis Guinness – their love, consistently positive support and open-minded approach to all religions paved the way for everything that has followed; my grandmothers, Geraldine and Grace – pioneers in their generation who rose above limitations and convention in the pursuit of their dreams; and my two sisters, Chloe and Lindis – special appreciation for all their love, and for lifelong friendship, encouragement, shared interests, and so many good memories…

The mystic selections in *Dawn has come* give a tiny hint of the extraordinary nature of a true spiritual teacher. The masters say "Love comes packaged as meditation" – so may the grace of daily effort remain with us to our very last breath!

EDITOR/TRANSLATOR

Anthea Guinness went to India on a 9-month Hindi scholarship and stayed for twenty-nine years. She studied, taught, translated – and copy-edited books on the bhakti tradition. With a PhD in comparative religion, she is the founder of Salt River Publishing and lives in Arizona.

SALT RIVER PUBLISHING

Salt River Publishing believes in encouraging artists and publishing professionals to come together and reach their empowered "Yes!"

Salt River was established as a no-profit publisher with the idea of helping writers, translators, poets, graphic artists and photographers bring their work into publishable form.

We provide links to a range of publishing professionals who offer services for anybody with a book in the making.

And we publish books that inspire and encourage, including ones that deepen the understanding of mysticism.

Do you have one?

www.SaltRiverPublishing.com

A TASTE OF SRP TITLES

The inner way

+ "**A beautiful collection** of unusual stories, inspiring poetry and fresh translations of ancient texts... By turns evocative, startling, deeply moving and delightful... I open this book and so often am moved to tears: it touches that deep place of yearning within." INNER WAY, responses

+ "As human beings we have a unique capacity: to expand our consciousness to its infinite potential. The mystics do not say this is easy. But they assure us it is possible..." INNER WAY, introduction

+ **A taste** of selections from more than 100 mystics: **Juan de la Cruz**, "On a night of darkness, enflamed by love and yearning – O happy chance! – I slipped away undetected, my house at last grown still…" **Shiv Dayal Singh**, "What a night! What an incredible, amazing night. I'm longing to tell someone – but who will know what I'm talking about? I saw, I tasted, the Root…" **Namdev**, "When I see him, I sing – that's how this nothing of a slave became tranquil, patient: when you meet the radiance of the true master, you merge in song…" **Chuang-tse**, "The purpose of words is to convey ideas. When the ideas are grasped, the words are forgotten. Where can I find a man who has forgotten words? He is the one I would like to talk to!" INNER WAY, excerpts

Stumbling towards enlightenment

• "Shanan Harrell has stumbled onto a writing style that is at the same time quirky and profound, witty and wise, insightful and delightful… Her book is about how to be better humans in spite of our bumbling, fumbling, grumbling selves… Engaging, a giggle fest and soul-searching all at the same time." STUMBLING TOWARDS ENLIGHTENMENT, responses

+ **A taste:** "I recently hiked the China Lake Naval Weapons Station Petroglyph Canyon. That is not a misprint."

+ **Taste 2:** "Several years back I was invited to a very hip, über-cool party of the yoga elite in my stomping grounds of Dallas, Texas. The invitation read: *Come Celebrate Randy's Moksha!* Randy's Moksha? Is it like a Bar Mitzvah? A psychic healing? Vasectomy reversal? Should I bring a covered-dish casserole? … (I saved my Frito Pie for another party.)"

+ **Taste 3:** "I don't remember where I first heard this particular bit of wisdom, but it's become a real favorite. I've tried to live by its high standard and I can't say I've always succeeded. I've passed it on to many and now I want to share with you this great universal precept – **Never** miss a good opportunity to shut up... So I practice the sacred art of shutting up. I remind myself to listen deeply to the other person, quiet myself, pay attention. It's a beautiful and humbling practice. And the opportunities, seriously, are endless. Now get out there and shut the hell up." STUMBLING TOWARDS ENLIGHTENMENT, excerpts

Community adventure

+ "**Long Dene** was one of a small number of schools that altered the whole intellectual climate of education in England... Pioneeers like the Guinnesses changed the face of the old Victorian notion of the role of education... This book paints a lively portrait of a child's dream school, housed in a castle with a lake and endless places to explore... Amazing to think the school existed as early as 1939, with organically grown food, naturopathic healthcare, and (for the staff!) home births assisted by the community's midwife…" COMMUNITY ADVENTURE, responses

+ **A taste:** One student remembers his first interview with John Guinness, founder and principal of the school: "The interview was conducted walking around the grounds in that lovely slow deliberate way he had. I felt here was a man who wouldn't panic if the whole place was on fire. He had a quiet air of confidence you could instantly respect."

+ The *Denizen* 1950 issue celebrates the triumph of building **a classic open-air amphitheatre** for dance, drama, music: This was a prodigious achievement, by student volunteers, under the direction of one of the teachers. A lot of the work was done during a summer heatwave and involved getting up before 6am to put in hard labour until 7.30, when daily housework took over until breakfast… COMMUNITY ADVENTURE, excerpts

Wake up! if you can

* "The sayings of Kabir in this book give a glimpse
  of what it is like to go beyond all our limitations
  and really wake up. And the sayings also give
  hints on how to do it – what is required along
  the way… The intention of this small book of
  sayings is to offer – thanks to Kabir – a home-
  opathic dose of hope, help and humour for the
  way. The sayings remind us, as a contemporary
  mystic once said, that the path is more long
  than hard." WAKE UP! IF YOU CAN, introduction

* **A taste:**

    If asleep, you dream of him;
    If awake, he's in your mind:
    Eyes so immersed, Kabir,
    You're conscious only of God –
    Never separate
    Even for a moment.

    WAKE UP! IF YOU CAN, excerpt

Dawn has come

+ "Paltu is the mystic who said about the path: 'In the game of love, whether heads or tails, it's God both ways: if I lose, I'm his – if I win, he's mine!' This saying and the songpoems of Paltu in *Dawn has come* remind us that the Naam bhakti path is a path of love – and in love, anything is possible."
  DAWN HAS COME, introduction

+ **A taste:**
  There's an upside-down well
  In the skies within
  Where a lamp is burning –
  A lamp is burning
  Without wick or oil...
  Dawn has come,
  A flute is playing in the skies:
  Mind – immersed, delighted...
  In the garden of Guru Gobind,
  Paltu blossomed
  Like a flower...

  DAWN HAS COME, excerpts

SALT RIVER BOOKLIST

- *The inner way: a mystic anthology of songpoems, stories, reflections* arranged with translations and notes by Anthea Guinness (SRP, 2013)
- *Stumbling towards enlightenment: a Yoga 101 collection* by Shanan Harrell (SRP, 2014)
- *Community adventure: the story of Long Dene School* by Sue Smithson (SRP, 2015)

Tuppany series
Translations of mystic writings by Anthea Guinness:
- *Wake up! if you can: sayings of Kabir* (SRP, 2014)
- *Dawn has come: songpoems of Paltu* (SRP, 2014)

www.SaltRiverPublishing.com

Published independently with Salt River assistance (editing, book design, cover design)

Books by Chloe Faith Wordsworth (Scottsdale, AZ: Resonance Publishing, 2007–2014):

* *Spiral up!* 127 *Energizing Options to be your best right now* (2014)
* *Quantum change made easy: breakthroughs in personal transformation, self-healing and achieving the best of who you are* (2007)
* *Empowering yourself with Resonance Repatterning*, and eleven other Resonance Repatterning practitioner books (2007–2014)

* *Dark bread and dancing: the diaries of Sue Rawson* by Rosemary Rawson (2013)

www.SaltRiverPublishing.com

COLOPHON

Typefaces: Adobe Brioso Pro (designed by Robert Slimbach), Vatican (designed by Alan Meeks), Adobe Jensen Pro (designed by Nicolas Jensen and Robert Slimbach)

Software: Adobe InDesign

Book Design and Composition: Carol White of Salt River Publishing (*email:* carol@saltriver publishing.com)

Cover Design: Carol White of Salt River Publishing (*email:* carol@saltriverpublishing.com)

Printer: createspace.com

Printing method: Print-on-Demand (POD) digital printing

Paper: Library quality

Binding: Perfect binding

AUTHORS NEED READERS

If you have enjoyed this Salt River book, please **recommend it** to your friends!

    Authors and artists publish their work because they want to share. **Readers** love new books. We invite **you** to take part in **lifting spirits** and **helping authors** attain their goal. 'The right words at the right time can turn a life around…'

* **give a copy** to friends – including your local library and study groups
* **write about it online** – emails, blogs, "like it" on social media, a candid review at Amazon

    Thank you from all of us – the writers, artists, editors and designers associated with the no-profit Salt River Publishing company.

www.SaltRiverPublishing.com

READER RESPONSE
TO SALT RIVER BOOKS

"So many problems are spiritual in nature. And healing often involves finding meaning, purpose and spiritual uplift. The right words at the right time can turn a life around. Therapists and practitioners can point the way for clients who are seeking meaning; writers and artists have an opportunity to share in that work. Thank you, Salt River."